KU-315-302

هل تحتفلين عندما تقومي بشيء كبير؟

Do you celebrate
when you do something great?

3

تستطعين أن تحتفلي بالشتاء.
You can celebrate winter.

احتفال
Celebrating

Gwenyth Swain

U/5 Bookbus

Aylestone
Library
0116 233

Arabic translation by Ahmed Al-Hamdi

small world

▲ Milet

For my grandfather Alfred P. Coman,
who knew how to celebrate the small things in life

To find out more about the pictures in this book, turn to page 22.
To find out more about sharing this book with children, turn to page 24.

The photographs in this book are reproduced through the courtesy of: © Trip/J. Sweeney, front cover; © Trip/G. Pritchard, back cover; Ling Yu, p. 1; Portland Rose Festival Association, Photo: Gayle Hoffman, p. 3; John S. Foster, p. 4; © Jeffrey J. Foxx, p. 5; Russell L. Ciochon, p. 6; © Trip/M. Jelliffe, p. 7; © John Elk III, p. 8; Ruthi Soudack, p. 9; Jeff Greenburg, pp. 10, 16; © Trip/B. Gibbs, p. 11; Lyn Hancock, p. 12; © Brian A. Vikander, p. 13; IPS, p. 14; © Trip/S. Grant, p. 15; © Elaine Little/World Photo Images, p. 17; Nancy Smedstad/IPS, p. 18; © Stephen Graham Photography, p. 19; © Trip/M. Ockenden, p. 20; Voscar, The Maine Photographer, p. 21.

Celebrating / Small World Series

Milet Publishing Ltd
6 North End Parade
London W14 0SJ
England
Email info@milet.com
Website www.milet.com

Second dual language edition, 2004
First English–Arabic dual language edition published by Milet Limited in 2000
All dual language editions published by arrangement with Carolrhoda Books, Inc., a division of Lerner Publishing Group, U.S.A.

Copyright © Carolrhoda Books, Inc., 1999

ISBN 1 84059 130 7

This book is sold subject to the condition that it shall not, by way of trade or otherwise, be lent, resold, hired out, reproduced, stored in a retrieval system, or transmitted in any form or by any means – electronic, mechanical, photocopying, recording, or otherwise – without the publisher's prior consent in any form or binding other than that in which it is published and without a similar condition, including this condition, being imposed upon it by the subsequent purchaser.

Printed in China

تستطعين أن تحتفلي بالربيع.

You can celebrate spring.

تحتلفين برحلة الى المتنزه

Celebrate a trip to the park

أو بـزيارة مـن الملك.

or a visit from the king.

عندما يحدث شيء ذو أهمية خاصة، رتبي
شعرك بطريقة جديدة.

When something special happens,
get a new hairdo.

ارتدوا أفضل ملابسكم. قوموا بشيءٍ لم
تفكروا القيام به من قبل أبداً!

Put on your best outfit. Do something
you never thought you'd do!

اركب على أكتاف أحد ما عندما تمر
المسيرة خلال المدينة.

Get on someone's shoulders
when a parade goes through town.

أو التحقنَّ بالناس الذين يمشون
في المسيرة ولوّحنَّ بالأعلام.

Or join the marchers
and wave a flag around.

عندما يبدو اليوم ذو أهمية خاصة، اضرب الطبل
When the day seems special,
bang a drum

أو أرقصي برقصة.

or dance a dance.

أو أركض بسباق.

Run a race.

انتهزوا الفرصة.

Take a chance.

يحتفل الناس بأشياء عديدة، الجديدة والقديمة.
People celebrate many things,
old and new.

هل هناك شيء تريدون أن تحتفلوا به، كذلك؟
Is there something
you want to celebrate, too?

فكروا بالوقت الذي تقضونه مع عائلتكم
Think of time you spend with family

أو الأيام التي تقضونها مع الأصدقاء.

or days you spend with friends.

احتلفوا بالعطلات وفي كل يوم.
Celebrate holidays and every day.

احتفلي في أي مكان كان، وفي أي وقت كان!
Celebrate no matter where,
no matter when!

More about the Pictures

Front cover: In North Korea, children celebrate the fiftieth anniversary of the Workers' Party.

Back cover: This girl is dressed up for the Notting Hill Carnival, which takes place in a West Indian neighbourhood in London, England.

Page 1: People in Taiwan celebrate with a parade.

Page 3: This girl in Portland, Oregon, celebrates winning a ribbon in a local parade.

Page 4: Winter snows make kids in Ruby, Alaska, smile.

Page 5: This boy in Georgia, a country in southeastern Europe, celebrates the coming of spring.

Page 6: It's time for fun at a park in Hanoi, Vietnam.

Page 7: An Ashanti chief visits during a festival in Ghana, a West African country.

Page 8: A girl in Mali, in West Africa, wears a new hairdo for a special day.

Page 9: For the Holi festival in India, people pour bright-coloured powder on their heads and celebrate the end of winter.

Page 10: You have to be tall to see what's going on in Saint Petersburg, Russia.

 **Page 11:** On a London street, English children wave their flag, the Union Jack.

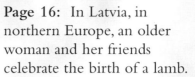 **Page 16:** In Latvia, in northern Europe, an older woman and her friends celebrate the birth of a lamb.

 **Page 12:** In Nunavut, a territory in northern Canada, a young Inuit child learns to play the drum.

 **Page 17:** Going to school is a good reason to celebrate for these children in Tokyo, Japan.

 **Page 13:** A girl in Laos, a country in Southeast Asia, dances a traditional dance to wish people well.

 **Page 18:** In Minneapolis, Minnesota, a grandmother and grandchild celebrate their Ukrainian heritage.

 **Page 14:** In Côte d'Ivoire, a country on the west coast of Africa, a young man takes part in a race.

 **Page 19:** Three friends enjoy just being together in Omaha, Nebraska.

 **Page 15:** To celebrate Thanksgiving, these American children dress up a little differently—as the Statue of Liberty.

 **Page 20:** Celebrating Halloween is popular with these children in London, England.

Page 21: A young girl celebrates summer in Quebec City, Canada.

A Note to Adults on Sharing This Book

Help your child become a lifelong reader. Read this book together, taking turns as you both read out loud. Look over the photographs and choose your favourites. Sound out new words and come back to them later for review. Then try these "extensions"—activities that extend the experience of reading and build discussion and problem-solving skills.

Talk about Celebrating

All around the world, you can find people celebrating. Discuss with your child the things people celebrate in different countries. What holidays, birthdays, and other events do you celebrate? How do your celebrations differ from celebrations in other parts of the world? How are they the same?

Plan Your Next Celebration

With your child, plan your next holiday, birthday, or other celebration. Ask your child what decorations will be needed. Make a list of foods you will need. Talk about inviting friends and family. Then work together to complete your plans and make this celebration special.